Barriers: social and economic exclusion in London

Social and economic exclusion remains a harsh reality for many Londoners in the 1990s. Through presenting key findings and highlighting major issues this pamphlet illustrates that the problems of exclusion are not amenable to simple and single solutions. ***Barriers*** *outlines recommendations which should be key to an anti-exclusion agenda for London involving all sectors.*

London pamphlet 2

London Voluntary Service Council

March 1998

British Library Cataloguing in Publication Data

A catalogue record for this book is available from the British Library

ISBN 1 872582 46 X

Typesetting: Jacki Reason, 29 Ella Road, London N8 9EL
Printing: Spider Web, 14 Sussex Way, London N7 6RS
Cover design: Jacki Reason

Published by LVSC, 356 Holloway Road, London N7 6PA

Photo credits: 999 Club, Tony Grummit, Elaine Kennedy, Tony Othen and Trevor Watling

Preface

Barriers provides a springboard for discussion on the ways in which a myriad of social and economic factors create and perpetuate the exclusion of many individuals and communities in London, and how all sectors can address them.

Economic and social exclusion is now more than ever on the political agenda. It was one of the issues prioritised by the new government, with the Social Exclusion Unit being set up to look at the causal factors of exclusion and the means by which they can be addressed. Work by the London Pride Partnership and the London Study underlines the need for an holistic approach to policies which purport to tackle social and economic exclusion. A future Greater London Authority and London Development Agency could provide a strategic role in tackling the exclusion, poverty and deprivation experienced by many Londoners. We hope this revised *Barriers* will play a role in bringing such an approach closer.

A small discussion group from London's voluntary sector identified themes of 'anti-discrimination', 'social inclusion', 'sustainability' and 'participation by those vulnerable to exclusion'. *Barriers* combines their thinking with up-to-date statistics and recommendations to provide a key to an anti-exclusion agenda for London.

LVSC would like to thank all those who contributed time, ideas and suggestions to the production of *Barriers.* Particular thanks are due to members of the voluntary sector advisory group, and to Grand Metropolitan plc, who sponsored the seminar in June 1996 from which *Barriers* emerged.

The findings presented in *Barriers* are drawn from a number of sources including the Association for London Government, the British Crime Survey, the Centre for Independent London Transport, the Child Poverty Action Group, the London Pride Partnership, the London Research Centre, the London TEC Council, London Youth Matters and various media reports.

Social and economic exclusion: a question of barriers

Barriers' starting point is that social and economic exclusion is not simply a matter of employment and income. There are innumerable ways in which people are denied access to inclusion into society and the benefits that this brings: barriers which create and perpetuate exclusion exist in all areas of life.

LVSC identifies nine barriers in this document:

- ❑ **Discrimination**
- ❑ **Poverty**
- ❑ **Employment**
- ❑ **Childcare**
- ❑ **Fear of crime**
- ❑ **Transport**
- ❑ **Education**
- ❑ **Health**
- ❑ **Housing**

Issues that arise in considering each of these barriers overlap. This is not simply repetition but illustrates how forms of social and economic exclusion reinforce each other. These are complex problems which may not be amenable to single solutions. In particular, inequality and discrimination on the grounds of race and ethnicity pervade all the other barriers, producing multiple disadvantage and reinforcing exclusion at every step. Anti-racist initiatives should be central to any coordinated anti-exclusion programme.

This list of barriers is not definitive. Neither are the recommendations. *Barriers* aims to contribute to a debate on the issues all sectors need to address. In addition to the nine identified barriers, the pamphlet describes how regeneration and development policy and the structure of London governance could positively impact on social and economic exclusion in the capital.

LVSC believes this can only happen through true cross-sector partnerships in London. We hope that *Barriers* will serve some purpose in promoting those partnerships.

The London dimension

London is a city of extremes. Although it is one of the ten richest regions in Europe, it is the region where poverty is growing at the fastest rate.

London has the highest average wage in the UK, with the number of people having an annual income in excess of £50,000 being twice that of the UK as a whole. Conversely, a fifth of the full-time adult workforce earns less than the Council of Europe's 'decency threshold'.

London suffers from the outside perception of being in the affluent south east of England, resulting in resentment when resources are targeted at the region. As a region, however, London has the advantage of having a developed voluntary sector infrastructure and a long history of social activism.

Research in London has revealed the social geography of poverty and exclusion in the city, identifying that the same areas (wards and boroughs) and the same social groups score highly on most indicators of deprivation, poverty and exclusion. In London averages count for little as accurate indicators of quality of life; for a true picture you need to take full account of the opposites of wealth and power.

The Joseph Rowntree Foundation 1995 *Inquiry into Income and Wealth*[1] identified a national trend towards a widening of income inequality, leading to endemic social and economic exclusion for a large minority. It warned that the '... failure to reintegrate this excluded minority into the mainstream of society will leave the well-to-do majority with a heavy price to pay in terms of increased public spending, wasted economic resources, and social dislocation.'

More recent research reveals how conditions in the capital epitomise that process with greater - and growing - inequality of income, health, life expectancy, educational and employment opportunities.

[1] *ISBN 1 85935 005 4; 2 volumes: £15.00*

Discrimination barriers

The varying impact the barriers identified in this paper has on particular social groups is neither accidental nor a mere by-product of global forces and local conditions.

Discrimination through the action and inaction of other citizens, employers, institutions and legal statute is at the heart of many people's experience of civic, social and working life.

London is one of the most cosmopolitan cities in the world. **Black and minority ethnic communities** are projected to make up 28% of London's population by 2011. For many working people, racial abuse and harassment remains 'part of the job'. Black people are more likely to be unemployed and are under-represented in many sectors and positions. Reports of 'racial incidents', rising by over 50% from 1988 to 1993, reflect the reality of racial discrimination.

Recommendations

❑ **Ensure commitment to eradicate discrimination, whether at work or in wider society, is pivotal to central and local government policy, and not simply an afterthought to attain a minimum equal opportunities standard.**

❑ **Analyse official statistics by gender, ethnicity, age and disability to monitor the impact of discrimination.**

❑ **Rigorously enforce and monitor the new racial harassment criminal offence.**

❑ **Encourage capacity building for Black and minority ethnic voluntary organisations and support for businesses.**

People with a disability are discriminated against in many ways, including through lack of physical access and unequal treatment at the workplace. The Disability Discrimination Act is an inadequate response to such issues, failing to confront countless incidents of discrimination faced by disabled people. Proposed plans to cut disability benefit will only further exclude people with disabilities from society, both socially and economically.

Recommendations

- ❑ **Introduce a Commission for Disabled People with enforcement powers.**
- ❑ **Enforce planning authorities and private sector contractors to deliver quality accessible public services.**
- ❑ **Investigate the possibility of a comprehensive disability income scheme.**

Lesbians and gay men face discrimination in the criminal law, social institutions and the armed forces, and in relation to parenting rights, as well as being exposed to harassment, abuse and violence. Existing UK legislation enshrines prejudice and discrimination.

Recommendations

- ❑ **Introduce an anti-discrimination law - including parenting rights - for lesbians and gay men.**
- ❑ **Equalise the age of consent.**
- ❑ **Introduce equal status for same sex couples.**
- ❑ **Repeal Section 28 of the 1988 Local Government Act.**

Women are more likely to be in poverty than men. They represent a large part of the workforce yet often receive less money for comparable work and are more likely to be in part-time or temporary work. Women are marginalised from participation in decision making. Many women live with the threat of violence and harassment.

Recommendations

- ❑ **Alter the tax and benefit systems to target poverty among women.**
- ❑ **Ensure equal rights for all workers, irrespective of work pattern or status.**

- ❏ **Instigate positive action, to enable more involvement in decision making.**

Age can be another factor in discrimination, for both younger and older people. Many young people receive less in benefit payments, exposing them to a greater risk of poverty and homelessness. Young people are not regarded as being able to participate in initiatives designed to assist them. Older people may have to cope with a lack of basic services such as shopping, cleaning and respite care as well as issues of physical access and pension levels. Age discrimination within employment is rife.

Recommendations

- ❏ **Encourage young people's involvement in crime prevention and regeneration programmes.**
- ❏ **Make appropriate funding available for care in the community and other support services for older people.**
- ❏ **Plan a coordinated approach to services, policies, access and free travel throughout London for older people.**
- ❏ **Introduce effective measures to combat employers' discrimination due to age.**

Refugees and asylum seekers are directly discriminated against by statute, compelling employers, institutions and services to discriminate against people due to refugee or asylum seeker status.

Recommendations

- ❏ **Implement an immediate review of asylum seeker legislation and guidance for employers, schools and service delivery.**
- ❏ **Argue for a more humane reception of refugees into 'Fortress Europe'.**

Poverty barriers

Research reveals the extent of poverty in the capital and its concentration in geographical areas and amongst certain groups, in particular Black and minority ethnic communities, lone parents, long-term unemployed people, women, pensioners and local authority and housing association tenants.

Living on a low income is key in determining the health and educational opportunities, housing conditions and quality of life of many people who experience social and economic exclusion. It also means a lack of resources to access services, goods and other opportunities. Poverty causes isolation, threatens membership of supporting networks, induces fear about the present and the future, causes stress, illness, low self esteem, a feeling of disjunction with one's surroundings, and a increased risk of being a victim of crime.

Key findings

- More than 2 million Londoners are living in, or on the margins of poverty
- The majority of those identified as being in poverty are also in work
- Average male full-time earnings in the City of London are £740 per week; in the neighbouring Spitalfields ward in Tower Hamlets there is 33% unemployment and 77% of children live in unsuitable accommodation
- 1 in 5 dependent children in London live in households with no wage earner

Issues

- Poverty is unequally spread through London, spatially and socially.
- People on low incomes increase the benefit bill and play a minor role in direct tax income, and are therefore unable to support a full range of local amenities and businesses.
- Low pay is as great a cause of poverty as unemployment.
- Poverty in an area affects the local economy, through lack of circulation of cash.

Recommendations

- **Set up credit unions as a means of financial help and a challenge to the growing presence of loansharks.**
- **Introduce smart card technology to enable concessionary travel and services without stigma or resentment.**
- **Implement an appropriate regional minimum wage designed to alleviate low wage poverty and have a positive impact on productivity.**

- ❑ **Encourage local economic regeneration to increase cash circulation in local economies and so ensure areas of severe deprivation do not slide into complete collapse, thus giving tax and rate relief for community businesses.**

- ❑ **Enable community economic development as the key to successful and sustainable regeneration initiatives., including local capacity building, to ensure that programmes thrive locally.**

- ❑ **Ensure a well-resourced, accessible, holistic advice service (including debt, money, social services, housing, asylum rights), is appropriately located and targeted at key groups - Black and minority ethnic communities, women and people with disabilities.**

Key findings

- ➤ London has a higher ratio of unemployed people (1:3) than the national average (1:4)
- ➤ Black and minority ethnic communities are almost 3 times more likely to be unemployed than white people
- ➤ Unemployment rates in the 10% of London wards with the highest rates were 11.9% to 22.5%, while over half of all London wards had unemployment rates below 6%
- ➤ In 1995 22% of London's female workforce were in low paid, part-time employment

Employment barriers

Long-term unemployment is unquestionably heavily connected with social and economic exclusion. The Government's Welfare to Work programme for unemployed people acknowledges the need for vocational training and real work experience, especially for young people. However, integration into the workforce is not by itself a guarantee of removing social exclusion - or indeed poverty. Low paid and insecure employment continues to grow as a feature of certain sectors of London's labour market.

A strategy to combat the exclusion of particular groups and areas from employment must consider the social barriers to obtaining and keeping employment. Equally, the macro economic factors that determine the availability and quality of jobs in the London economy should be identified.

A concentration on employment at the expense of other social factors will neither address the root of many people's exclusion, nor aid integration into the workforce.

Wider costs

- ❑ The collective costs of high benefit spending, wasted human resources and minimal direct tax income to central government is unquestionable.

- Wider social problems are associated with high levels of unemployment, especially with long-term and youth unemployment.

- Unemployed people's exclusion is compounded through missing out on in-work training (where most skills training in the UK takes place).

Issues

- The insecure and lower paid sector of the labour market continues to grow. Consequently, moving off benefit and into work represents a high risk option with little obvious reward.

- Employment is no guaranteed escape from poverty. The majority of people identified as being in poverty are also in work.

Recommendations

- **Remove some of the penalties associated with moving from benefit into work to give confidence to those to take temporary or insecure work.**

- **Design training programmes to match the needs of particular groups to those sectors of the economy likely to provide jobs, as part of generally accessible lifetime education programmes.**

- **Provide affordable, flexible, reliable and high quality childcare.**

- **Collect data - including aspirations - on the local employment situation for target groups, especially minority ethnic groups.**

- **Establish a regional minimum wage.**

- **Consider job creation as a key to reviving local economies and communities when setting up regeneration initiatives.**

Childcare barriers

Lack of childcare is a barrier which affects access to work, education and training, recreation and travel. It also reduces the possibility of maintaining contacts and networks, which can be the source of employment information.

The Government's commitment to a National Childcare Strategy is certainly a step forward. However, plans for after school clubs, nursery places for all four year olds and making childcare a priority for Single Regeneration Budget initiatives needs to go further. Commitment should be made to a strategy of universally available, affordable childcare for all families.

Key findings

- Only 41% of lone parents in the UK are employed - with only 17% employed full time; in France, 82% of lone parents work - 67% full time
- Local authority childcare services have fallen by 21.5% since 1982
- A national means tested subsidy of under 5s childcare would cost about £160m
- In one area in London 39% of 11 year olds look after themselves during the school holidays while their parents are at work
- The four UK local authority areas with the highest rates of lone parenthood are all in London - Lambeth (45% of families with dependent children), Southwark (43%), Islington (42%) and Hackney (41%)

Wider costs

- Employers with childcare support retain 80% of mothers after maternity leave. Those without achieve only a 30% return, with a resulting loss of skills and experience. Childcare can therefore result in savings on recruitment - through encouraging women to stay in post - fewer days lost through sickness and absenteeism, and positive publicity as a good employer.
- Research argues that childcare for pre-school children assists social and educational development in early years and helps ensure educational achievement. It also suggests a potential reduction in the incidence of accidents, vandalism and crime among school age children, with significant cost savings.

Issues

- Childcare assistance should be available to *all* parents.
- Children have the right to leisure and play, and to cultural and artistic activities.
- Safe, reliable childcare benefits the whole community.

Recommendations

- **Encourage employers to pursue family friendly employment policies, including flexible working, childcare assistance and ensuring that parents - especially lone parents - do not face discrimination.**

- **Introduce quality standards for childcare provision in London - agreed by all sectors - with indicators, targets and Kitemark type rewards.**

- **Encourage after school and holiday projects, and make it easier to change the use of premises to house them.**

Key findings

- Between 1981 and 1993 violent crime in London increased by more than 130%
- Black and minority ethnic communities are more likely to be victims of crime than white people
- 23% of young offenders say having a job would stop them offending; 13% say sport; 11% other leisure activities; 10% prison; 10% meeting victims
- Between 1% and 2% of the population - largely women and older people - never go out after dark due to fear of crime

Fear of crime barriers

While there may be no simple and direct causal link between high unemployment, poverty and crime, it is impossible to deny some connection. Social and economic trends contribute to increases in crime and undermine efforts to reduce it.

The increased risk of crime is concentrated among those who were already at risk. Minority ethnic groups feature heavily among those most vulnerable to crime, in particular younger people and those in inner city areas. This factor should be borne in mind when assessing Londonwide figures.

Crime rates can be reduced through a range of preventative measures. There is a need to identify and address the underlying social causes of offending and influence the attitudes of those likely to offend; to encourage behaviour changes away from crime.

Wider costs

- Home insurance in London is expensive in general and impossible to obtain in certain areas. This impacts on Londoners across all social groups, but penalises those in the most deprived areas and adversely affects attempts to create mixed tenure districts.

- The lack of people out after dark in some areas of London due to fear of crime has negative consequences for local services and retailers.

- Police spend £660 million a year on juvenile crime; three out of five 10-17 year olds are only cautioned.

Issues

- ❑ Penal deterrence has failed as a policy. A more sophisticated and varied social policy approach is needed to combat criminality and promote community safety.
- ❑ Labour market conditions and the incidence of crime are linked.
- ❑ Zero tolerance policing and fast track juvenile criminal processes are no substitute for young people being involved in the design and provision of diversionary activities.
- ❑ Pupils who under-perform at school are more likely to engage in anti-social behaviour.

Recommendations

- ❑ **Give priority to community initiatives such as improved estate housing management methods, youth action projects, neighbourhood mediation schemes and mentoring projects, as well as community crime prevention initiatives.**
- ❑ **Encourage safe community transport schemes to alleviate isolation and fear of being out after dark.**
- ❑ **Ensure pre-school provision is available.**
- ❑ **Put effort into initiatives aimed at improving school attendance and reducing the risk of disaffection, instead of exclusions.**

Transport barriers

The extent to which transport features as a barrier which causes and perpetuates social and economic exclusion is all too often glossed over. Much public transport is physically inaccessible and feels unsafe at certain times of the day. For certain groups, it is inadequate in many areas of London (including those of significant poverty) and is prohibitively expensive for people on low incomes.

The debate on the future of London's transport system continues to focus on how it feeds commuters directly into central London or on

Key findings

- More than half of London's 800,000 disabled people cannot use public transport due to difficulties with access
- Travel in London costs 20% more than in Paris and Berlin and 68% more than in Rome
- London Underground Ltd has reduced staff by 25% over the last five years
- Of the poorest 10% of households in London, 80% do not have a car

points of embarkation for tourists and business people. Little consideration is given to outer London journeys or equality issues. Transport is identified by all sectors as a key element in improving conditions in the capital. This is true for both urban regeneration of deprived areas and London's economic competitiveness.

The Government's proposals for a Greater London Authority emphasise the need for a London Transport Authority to provide a coordinated response to the capital's transport needs. A strategy for London transport is urgently needed and should prioritise issues of access, equality, safety and cost.

Wider costs

- ❑ Local and health authorities pick up large transport bills for hospital and special needs transport and the home delivery of non-acute services.
- ❑ There is growing public concern at the levels of traffic congestion and pollution in the capital; urgent action is needed to combat the effect this has on Londoners' health.
- ❑ A step-free London Underground would increase mobility impaired passengers' use by approximately 5% and therefore also increase revenue. It could also increase use by people with children, heavy shopping, luggage etc.
- ❑ Access problems caused by automated ticket barriers means high staffing levels in the station ticket hall, which has financial implications for London Underground and takes staff off the platforms.

Issues

- ❑ Public transport is seen as threatening and unsafe, especially at night.
- ❑ Transport issues and environmental concerns need to be considered together.
- ❑ London, with its dispersed jobs, training and education facilities, medical facilities and cultural centres presents complex, varied and expensive journeys.

- Unemployed people and those on low income either cannot afford to use public transport or spend a disproportionate amount of their income on travel.

Recommendations

- **A Greater London Authority needs to prioritise a comprehensive transport strategy.**

- **Encourage Community Safe Transport schemes, which benefit many people who feel unsafe on public transport - eg lone women and older people, particularly from minority ethnic communities.**

- **Improve access to stations and introduce more low level buses to remove the barriers of public transport to those with a disability.**

- **Guarantee free travel for older and disabled people.**

- **Consider smart card technology as a way of removing physical obstructions such as ticket barriers and the stigma of concessionary fares or debit travel accounts for job seekers.**

- **Introduce and monitor increased ridership for people with disabilities and lone women at night as a quality measure on all public transport.**

- **Carry out risk assessments out on all forms of public transport and at all points of access.**

Education barriers

A number of factors, including the disappearance of long-term secure employment, have contributed to a disaffection from societal institutions. This process begins with the education system and has resulted in a pattern of under achievement among large sections of young people.

Many young people drift in and out of school, further education and training programmes, finding it difficult to sustain the motivation to learn and develop. These patterns feed low self esteem and lead to a view of education and training as being of marginal value and compulsory training as something to be avoided. The Government's emphasis on education and life-time learning needs to be more than targets and league tables.

Key findings

- 2,250 children were permanently excluded from London schools in 1996 - one fifth of the national total
- Black students are excluded from school at the rate of 6:1 compared with white students
- Nine out of ten excluded pupils are boys
- A fifth of London's pupils do not have English as the main language spoken at home
- An estimated 1 in 4 street crimes in London are carried out by children during school hours

Issues

- London has a skill problem: a polarisation as well as shortage. Forty-two per cent of all vacancies are described as 'hard to fill', one third of all recruitment difficulties (especially in the IT field) are due to skill deficiencies.
- The UK has fallen to 42nd place in the educational competitiveness league. The average score given by business people, when asked to assess on a scale of 1 to 10 how well the education system met the needs of a competitive economy, was 2.79.
- Working class students have been identified as under-performing across all ethnic groups.
- Exclusion from school can lead to a dissociation from society, and there is a startling increase in the number of children excluded from primary schools.
- 'Employability' is identified with aspirations and values that need developing as pre-vocational training.

Recommendations

- **Extend and target mentoring projects for those young people identified as being in danger of 'going off the rails'.**
- **Coordinate childcare, pre-school, nursery, after-school, youth provision and mainstream education provision.**
- **Make available prevocational education and training to those most marginalised from the workforce.**
- **Establish and develop anti-truanting initiatives.**
- **Encourage partnerships between schools and businesses to give schools a better idea of what skills (especially IT) are needed by business and enable students to see examples, even role models, of the working population.**

- **Establish modular training programmes with measurable learning outcomes on which many young people can build.**

- **Make available effective, free opportunities for life-long learning, with childcare provision for unemployed people.**

- **Widen and strengthen adult education provision.**

Health barriers

Social and economic inequalities, demographic factors and inadequate and fragmented health service provision have a major impact on the health of Londoners and their access to health care. Poor health and access to services is linked with other variables such as poverty, homelessness and discrimination.

London has a high number of people with severe mental illness - especially in inner London - homeless and poorly housed people, people with drug problems, and people with HIV and AIDS. There are growing numbers of refugees and asylum seekers. All these groupings suffer more from ill health, and face particular difficulty accessing appropriate health care, as do older people, people with disabilities and people from Black and minority ethnic communities. High population mobility makes continuity of care and access to services more difficult.

Primary care services are underdeveloped, especially in deprived areas. Hospital and community health services are inadequate for the needs of London's population. Inadequate and costly transport make accessing these services difficult.

Wider costs

- A lack of preventative care or early intervention leads to greater health service costs later. Poor access to primary care services increases the pressure on hospital services, especially emergency services, to the detriment of all Londoners.

- Poor health represents a major waste of human resources, affecting people's ability to obtain and retain employment and contribute to community activity.

Key findings

- Between 1981 and 1991 mortality rates in London's most deprived wards increased by 8.4%, while rates in the most affluent wards decreased
- Over 20% of London GPs work single-handed compared with 11% nationally; they receive deprivation payments for 57% of their lists (10% nationally); 21% of inner London GPs have lists of over 2500 patients (8% nationally); almost one third have no practice nurse (10% nationally)
- Since 1990, 14% of London's acute hospital beds and 20% of elderly care beds have been lost
- By 2011, 17% of people over 65 in London will be from Black and minority ethnic communities

- There is a significant social cost in failing to provide adequate support for people with serious mental illness or substance misuse problems.

Issues

- Responsibility for health service planning and provision is fragmented between NHS Executive regional offices, health authorities and NHS trusts, with no one agency taking a Londonwide strategic overview of health needs and provision.

- There is no mechanism for inter-agency collaboration in promoting health; linking health with, for example, social services, transport, education, housing or environment.

- London's health services are seriously under-resourced and are currently facing further cutbacks in funding. There is insufficient voluntary and statutory sector provision to enable people to access health services such as interpreting.

- Inadequate funding of social services, and of other services such as housing and transport, has an impact on Londoners' health.

- There is little scope for voluntary organisations or local people to influence the planning and provision of health services.

Recommendations

- **Establish a publicly accountable, adequately funded strategic health authority for London, to plan, coordinate and monitor health services, and facilitate collaborative working between the statutory sector, users and carers, citizens and the voluntary sector.**

- **Adequately fund health services, to take account of the diversity and special needs of London's population.**

- **Make available sufficient resources to support and develop primary care.**

- **Guarantee Londoners equal access to high quality health services, for example through improved physical access, transport, information in appropriate formats and languages, advocacy and interpreting support.**

- **Ensure Health Improvement Programmes reflect the needs of all local people, including vulnerable groups.**

- **Introduce effective mechanisms to enable voluntary sector and user involvement in influencing primary care commissioning, developing and monitoring health improvement programmes, and Londonwide strategic health planning.**

Housing and homelessness barriers

Key findings

- 2.5% of white households are in overcrowded conditions compared with 16.9% of Black African households, 22.8% of Pakistani households and 53.8% of Bangladeshi households
- Inner London local authority housing departments accept 10,000 as homeless a year
- Housing benefit for single people aged 16 to 24 is restricted to the average cost of shared accommodation in the area identified by the local authority housing department, regardless of whether shared accommodation is available or appropriate
- Around 300 people sleep rough on the streets of inner London each night; one in four is aged under 25 years

The benefit trap is at its most punitive with regard to housing benefit. The previous government's policy of high rent and low benefit, coupled with the alternative of low paid, insecure employment, combine to ensure that many people relying on housing benefit will be unable to consider seriously taking the first step back into employment. This is especially true when dependent children are involved.

Residence in social housing has become an indicator of deprivation. With the overwhelming majority of new social housing tenants in receipt of income benefit, and stuck there, the attitude of 'if you get on, you get out' becomes entrenched.

Wider costs

- Large areas of single tenure social housing can amplify issues of social dislocation into issues of social unrest with disastrous consequences for local economies.

- The visibility of street homelessness in London undermines the development of one of London's key economic sectors through loss of tourism and inward investment.

- Homelessness, often combined with unemployment, substance misuse and poor health, adds significant costs to London.

Issues

- London is badly hit by a combination of housing benefit policy, high rents and the steep benefit taper.

- Inner London remains a draw for young homeless people.
- Black and minority ethnic housing associations can find it difficult to compete with larger housing associations.
- While much temporary accommodation may not be the most suitable, changes in housing benefit restrictions and bed and breakfast regulations have taken a great deal of temporary (and autonomous) bed spaces out of the equation.

Recommendations

- **Give substantial assistance to local Tenant Management of Housing schemes, which are seen to be successful in reducing criminality and the fear of crime, and improving the services to tenants.**
- **Support Black and minority ethnic housing associations so that housing associations can flourish as responsive community initiatives instead of a substitute for housing departments.**
- **Promote mixed tenure areas through physical regeneration of the area and also support for people led initiatives.**
- **Use a strategic approach to stem the flow of young people onto the capital's streets.**
- **Identify full housing options, as a key part of an holistic independent advice service.**
- **Simplify the process of obtaining permission for change of use of a building**
- **Make empty accommodation more easily available.**

Community involvement

User and community involvement is a key organising principle for the voluntary sector . It is the basis for the sector 's claim to be closer to those communities and groups which experience social and economic exclusion and more able to articulate their concerns than other sectors.

Community involvement is not the sole property of the voluntary sector . It belongs at the heart of decision making in London, especially in the opportunities present in **regeneration, development** and **governance**.

Regeneration

The Single Regeneration Budget (SRB) combined over 20 existing funding programmes from central government to create community-based urban regeneration projects via cross-sector partnerships. In the first round only 22% of successful bids had voluntary and community organisations as partners. The second round saw the figure rise to 44%; by the third round it was 56%. There has also been a welcome increase in the number of successful bids which have Black or minority ethnic agencies as partners. The overall level of community involvement remains too low, however, with over a third of bids in round 3 without voluntary or community sector partners.

Alongside this situation lies the perceived failure of most urban programmes to tackle the symptoms of urban deprivation. This can be attributed in large part to the absence of local people's direct involvement. High quality community involvement rather than nominal partnerships is the precondition for success.

The fourth round of SRB has seen a worrying decline in regeneration resources overall. London in particular appears to be losing out. Current Department of the Environment formulae for the allocation of funding has meant London receiving £220 million less than might have been the case, with other formulae using population and the index of local conditions, as well as other factors, impacting on the capital.

Local community involvement

It is essential that regeneration projects are designed in an holistic fashion and adopt a commitment to equal opportunities. Wide consultation and involvement encourages ownership and sustainability in regeneration projects, ensuring that the benefit reaches target communities and continues for the full funded timescale and beyond.

Local capacity building and the transfer of assets into the community are key factors in enabling local ownership in real and sustainable partnerships. Ownership and sustainability should be the first consideration in the design of a successful partnership initiative. Sustainable regeneration should encompass environmental, as well as social and economic factors.

Access to decision making structures and to the benefits of regeneration should be available to all members of the community, including disabled people, women, Black and minority ethnic communities, and other marginalised groups.

Urban programmes must address the needs of women and involve women in the development and implementation of schemes at every level, ensuring participation beyond the expression of community concerns and representation at decision making levels. Women play key roles in initiating community projects and voicing concerns through them. The absence of these women at the 'decision' stages confirms inadequate community involvement.

Young people are often presented as part of the problem within inner city areas and rarely as part of the solution. As a result they have little opportunity to contribute to regeneration strategies and make a real difference within their communities. Many training initiatives which target young unemployed people fail to attract young people. This could be avoided by the genuine involvement of young people in planning and implementing regeneration initiatives.

Lack of consultation and lack of experience of negotiating with key players in the regeneration field, and the appearance of a fragmented approach to regeneration by Black communities, has limited their involvement in regeneration. The impact of regeneration projects is still not being felt by most Black and minority ethnic communities, especially since the end of ringfenced funding. Standard mainstream policy initiatives will not automatically benefit minority ethnic communities unless specific targeting measures are taken.

A London development agency

Government plans for regional development agencies could offer greater community involvement in developing prosperity and sustainable growth for London.

The core function of London's forthcoming development agency will be to develop and implement regional economic strategies. Social exclusion must be top of the Agency's agenda, along with economic competitiveness. A cross-sector partnership representing

Londonwide networks and communities is vital if the long-term development needs of Londoners are to be met. In this way the expertise of voluntary and community groups can be best utilised, to ensure that London's development benefits all, and not just the few.

London governance

The discrimination, poverty and social exclusion identified in *Barriers* are compounded by a civic exclusion - the marginalisation of communities and groups from political decision making in London.

An LVSC questionnaire sent to over 22,000 voluntary organisations showed overwhelming support for the creation of a Greater London Authority (GLA). In no small measure this support was for an authority committed to addressing social exclusion across London and across the different barriers we have identified here.

The creation of a GLA is a chance to tackle this democratic deficit at the heart of London's civic life. It will not be able to achieve this by itself. However, it could be the centre of a vastly expanded political circle in which those communities who have had no say in and felt least benefit from London's prosperity, find a powerful voice, especially on those issues which have greatest impact on their lives.

A strategic authority

The setting up of the Government's Social Exclusion Unit gives some indication of how the GLA should approach social and economic exclusion in the capital. Social exclusion has complex causes and demands complex solutions which might cut across areas of the GLA's competence.

The new authority needs to be imbued with a mission to look across all its areas of functional responsibility and explore ways in which strategic planning in all its areas of competence can have positive spin-offs for excluded communities. It is vital that each of its functional areas should be able to account for their contribution to fighting social exclusion in London.

A democratic authority

The overriding general principle must be that the GLA is directly accountable to the people of London through regular election. However, in itself, this may not be enough to achieve the explosion of civic participation needed to tackle London's democratic deficit. New ways must be found to involve local and interest communities in the governance of London.

LVSC proposes a Civic Forum for London, bringing together different sectors and communities in an attempt to generate solutions to London's problems. As well as building on London's 'partnership' experience a Civic Forum could make civic participation more relevant and accessible to all Londoners. Universities, voluntary organisations, trades unions, faith communities, disability groups, Black and minority ethnic communities, young people, business associations, community groups and many others, working together to common agendas, would be able to identify the complexity of barriers and generate imaginative solutions to them.

Barriers to involvement in 'political' activity are well known: costs of travel and childcare, fatigue induced by poverty and a succession of failed community initiatives, loss of contact with the workplace and the language of decision making can all mitigate against involvement in civic activity.

London's new political structures will need to reflect an inclusive political culture. Initiatives such as a Civic Forum will ensure that a lean GLA has the exponential expansion of civic participation foremost in its mind at all times.

Breaking down the barriers - a partnership response

Conclusions

Social and economic exclusion remains a harsh reality for many Londoners in the 1990s. Through presenting key findings and highlighting major issues *Barriers* has illustrated that the problems of social and economic exclusion in London are not amenable to simple and single solutions.

Many of the recommendations in the pamphlet would require new legislation to tackle the worst discrimination; some demand considerable financial investment, others would require the adoption of simple non-excluding practices.

In order to break down the barriers to participating fully in society faced by a growing number of London's population, in order to combat poverty, deprivation and discrimination, a partnership response is clearly required. The complexity of the issues involved carries a number of simple truths:

- ❑ No one agency or sector is able to eliminate any one barrier identified in this paper; partnership and collaboration are prerequisites.
- ❑ No one agency or sector has sufficient knowledge or expertise to determine what it is that partnerships and collaboration need to achieve.
- ❑ No one agency or sector is able to provide long-term, sustainable solutions to the great majority of the issues raised in this pamphlet without the involvement of the people who are intended to benefit.

Voluntary and community organisations occupy a unique position with regard to many of those groups and communities most vulnerable to social and economic exclusion. They are able to act as amplifiers for those voices which are the least heard in the many papers, reports and conferences that proliferate on social and economic exclusion.

Any agency in any sector which takes seriously the need to combat social and economic exclusion in London must ensure that the intended beneficiaries are not themselves excluded from involvement in the design of initiatives, programmes, schemes and projects.

Breaking down the barriers for London's excluded population must be a priority for the new Greater London Authority, should it be created. A partnership across the commercial, public and voluntary sectors is vital to the success of any anti-exclusion initiative.

Only then can the issues highlighted in *Barriers* be fully addressed and the daily plight faced by many Londoners begin to be overcome.

Established in 1910, London Voluntary Service Council strengthens London's 30,000 voluntary organisations by providing them with support services and giving them a loud and clear voice on issues that affect Londoners.

This pamphlet – the second of a series on London issues – was written by Adam Scorer and Kate Jarman, both from LVSC's Policy Department.

If you have any comments or would like to contribute to the debate please write to Kate Jarman, LVSC, 356 Holloway Road, London N7 6PA

Pamphlet no 1 – *Enriching democracy: a Civic Forum for London* – sets out the case for a Civic Forum for London.